WHEN
THE DARK
SPOKE
TO ME

Andrews McMeel Publishing
a division of Andrews McMeel Universal
1130 Walnut Street, Kansas City, Missouri 64106

www.andrewsmcmeel.com

22 23 24 25 26 VEP 10 9 8 7 6 5 4 3 2 1

ISBN: 978-1-5248-7391-2

Library of Congress Control Number:

Editor: Samantha Jones
Editor: Katie Gould
Art Director: Holly Swayne
Designer: Sierra S. Stanton
Production Editor: Jasmine Lim
Production Manager: Julie Skalla

ATTENTION: SCHOOLS AND BUSINESSES

Andrews McMeel books are available at quantity discounts with bulk purchase for educational, business, or sales promotional use. For information, please e-mail the Andrews McMeel Publishing Special Sales Department: specialsales@amuniversal.com.

WHEN THE DARK SPOKE TO ME

Christabelle
Marbun

Andrews McMeel
PUBLISHING®

"That's the thing about pain. It demands to be felt."

—John Green, *The Fault in Our Stars*

*Dedicated to the Fireflies that hold my Knowledge,
Victories I see in May, and the Bravery that never left me.*

Trigger Warning:
This book contains themes of
Death and suicidal ideation,
reader discretion advised.

Death

/deTH/

noun

    1.   My first love

I had never known Life
until I had loved Death to exhaustion.

Stories,
They end all the time right?

To the rest of the world,
Death was reckless.
But to me,
She was everything I needed.

So did Death choose us,?
or did Life simply state that Death would
be a better fit for a world who hardly
understands it?

I have come to learn
that there are many
who don't like killing
but enjoy the thought
of taking a life.

I can't feel the touch of your gravestone;
I can't leave roses by the grass.
But I hope you know that
the second week of every December,
I quietly miss you.

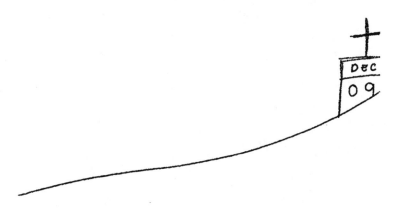

I thought it selfish for you to leave;
I treated seeing Death as a choice.
It was unfair, but it was all I could do.
I know now that you never wanted to
leave, you just wanted to see an old friend.

My Dearest Death,

Thank you for loving me
when life didn't.

— Your secret admirer

Loving Death was the easiest thing in the world;
I never needed to worry about Her leaving.

But justifying our love was a much
different story. It was mocked, insulted,
they assumed I was mad.

But they had never met Her.
They had never felt Her warm touch,
Her kind gaze, and the sense of security
one would feel around Her.

She was the unknown and people feared
the unknown. They hated Her, assigned
Her to darkness.

Yet it never bothered Her. Humanity
seemed like playful little children.

I saw Her and loved Her.
And it was the easiest thing in the world.

I slashed around in the dark,
fearing something would hurt me.
Finally, after blindly cutting the darkness,
I hit something. I thought it was over; the monster
was gone. But instead, I felt my arms sting, I heard
droplets hit the floor, dense and heavy with guilt.
The familiar scent of iron caught me off guard.
I sat in silence, now realizing this was what I
was meant for all this time. The girl who became
friends with the darkness by giving her life to it.

And yet Life was far less than what I was promised it would be. The sickly-sweet lies dripped off his tongue like poisonous honey. I danced into his tricks and siren songs. But even then, I could not leave his grasp, although I loved another, I could not escape. So I will sit here, stroking his hair, hoping I do not anger him with regret filling my eyes.

—Requiems of a toxic love.

The world seemed to fit perfectly in His fingertips, but the world wasn't Life's to hold. He had ripped it out of a past lover. Yet Death, compassionate as ever, would kindly smile. For She knows that in the end, She will have her chance to embrace all of us once again.

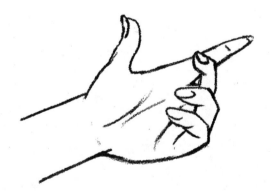

I sat once again in my bed,
A place I've seen myself die many times,
And yet, She does not come for me.

Losing them felt like my shadow was
pulled out from underneath me.
It felt like the worst kind of sabotage.

I don't understand, how do you breathe?
How do you wake up every morning and
be just fine with this kind of loss?
How do you live ignoring the fact that I could have died?

Am I truly that disposable to you?
Am I truly that disposable to you?

The urge to see an old friend has me
anxiously waiting by the door.
I was young, proud of myself for being
just tall enough to reach the doorknob.
My best friend was coming today;
everything needed to be perfect.
My eyes light up as I hear a gentle knock on the
door, I rush to open it.
"Hello, Death! It's been a while,
please come in."

I knew I was on borrowed time the
minute Death appeared at my door.

If it were up to me,
I would have the darkness stay,
And make sure the light could
Never take anything away from
me ever again.

I can only hope that one day my
bathroom floor will accept me,
the pill bottles will hold my hand,
and the wailing sirens of the blue
and red lights will leave me be.

I only missed you when I was dying.

I fear that I have not made enough
memories for Death to let me in.

Now that I've seen where our love ends,
I wish the destination was not part of the
journey at all.

Life was never kind to
the mistresses of Time.

The breaking of skin followed by the
sting of childhood memories is often the kind of
euphoric pain that cannot
be defeated.

I started to get sick of
Missing days,
Missing fights,
Missing you,
And missing nights.
So I stood up,
walked away,
and threw my soul,
into the night.

I looked Life right in his eyes, daring Him to stop me. I rattled the bottle in front of Him, tempting Him to deny the fact that I could be reunited with Death in a matter of minutes. Everything I needed to end it all was right between my fingers. But I will not let my pride overtake me this time. I gently set the bottle on the counter, opened the bathroom door, and walked away from the thing I wanted most.

"Well, well, well,"
I said,
"To what do I owe the pleasure?"

She smiled, silent in her secrets. I bring over a tray for some tea, ushering Her to sit down.

"Another already? So soon."
— I missed you

I gently pick up the teapot to pour her favorite cup of chamomile tea. I lightly laugh under my breath, who knew Death's favorite tea would be chamomile?
why wouldn't it be?

"None for me, my visit will be quick."

I pause my pouring, finally meeting Her eyes. We both know no one else has already packed their bags for Death.

"After all this time?"

She takes my hand and holds my cheek,

"Yes, my love. We can be together now."

If I could hold them I would,
If I could tell my younger self
That they're not alone I would.
If I were allowed to unlock
The door for them I would,
To let them out of the darkness,
And back into a world that would
Never hurt them again.
If I could unbury my childhood,
I would.
But alas, I can do nothing more than
Stand here and mourn for something
I never had.

Did you think I wanted to hear it?
That I wanted to feel the heartbeat
of my childhood stop so abruptly?
Did you think I enjoyed washing the
blood of laughter that once left my lips off my hands?
I never wished for this.
But she needed to die,
                    she was too sweet, too kind,
                         too
                              hopeful.
It was right to spare her, better, even. She deserved
the world, one that she could love freely in. We needed to
survive, and this was the only way.
I still mourn for her, but in the end,
she needed to die so that we could live.

After years of being hurt
by His hand,
I finally understood,
Life had never cared
For the recklessly in love.

How many more times must
the world fall on me before
it realizes that it created
me to be mortal?

— A SOUL LIKE ATLAS

I thought I knew exactly how I would
grieve, I thought I was ready to fight the big wave that
would crash over me. But when grief came knocking, I
was hit with overwhelming silence.
No screaming, no fighting, no tears.
Just quiet.
That was the day I learned to
hate the silence.

I wasn't trying to give in,
but the siren songs of Death
could not keep me
from coming towards Her.
Not after the way
Life has hurt me.

Death drove 150 on the highway. She knew nothing of slowing down. Time was a good friend to Her, and tonight, time had given her the keys. We passed through memories and moments yet to happen; I marveled at their beauty. I slowly calmed myself, quietly sinking into the passenger seat, feeling the vibration of the car go against my whole being. Death was in no hurry; She never is. Those who think that She arrives too soon simply underestimate her punctuality. She is not reckless; She simply does not treat us like fragile little beings. Not even Love could stand against Her. At the end of the night, as the sun crept through the mountains, She dropped me off by my doorstep. I am filled with thrilling exhaustion. It feels as though centuries have passed, but Death has a funny way of defining my mortality.

You could ask me why I did it, why I decided to finally write my last letter. And although the rest of the world tried its best to wrestle the pen away from me, in the end, I still signed my name. I don't know why I did it. I don't know why the bathroom floor was so inviting that night. All I know is that one minute I was alive, and the next I was—

The Bad has always kept
its distance from Good,
why? For the very reason
that Bad was Good's oldest friend,
with the vastest knowledge
of its secrets.

I envy the daughters who had the chance
to hold their father's hand without the
fear that he might *never* let go.

How do you deal with
a grief that never
hurt you?

I was finally able to breathe.
For the first time, inhaling was an option.
But before my lungs could dance with the air,
everything went dark. And suddenly, I could feel
my lungs no further.

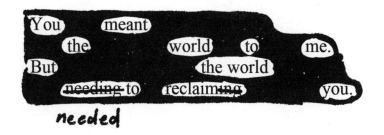

You meant
the world to me.
But the world
needing to reclaiming you.

needed

She was one of the most important things to her. The one thing the rest of the world was not allowed to touch. She was Death's poet, and she took pride in it.

Yet I do not think I would regret
spending my life being so
occupied with Death.

My fear of losing my loved ones to Death started to fade the moment I met Her. Now I know that I can let go of their hands; I know they would soon hold Hers.

I have come to learn that the Darkness never alters, our eyes simply start to adjust themselves to such horrors.

I thought the world of you,
but one day, the world ended on the
corners of my bathroom walls.

It's so fascinating to me that people can move on after the death of a loved one. That kind of loss, that kind of insufferable pain, how can a heart possibly heal from that? How does it mend itself after having its strings cut?
Look at you, look at your heart.
How resilient you are.

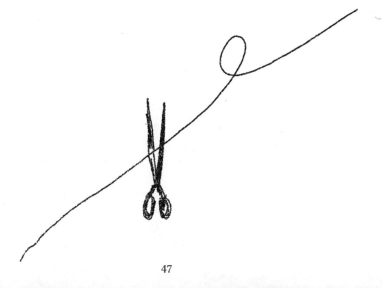

It's a shame to know that someone grew accustomed to their tomb for the sake of eternal beauty.

Oh, the things Death would do just to
have you. Yet here you are, every day,
politely declining. Telling Her that when you are
ready, you will join Her.

Whether it be the loss of a person,
the loss of a love, or the loss of one's soul, I hope you
know that She's kept your lesson away for safekeeping.
And if you ask her kindly, Death will gladly give them to
you when you're ready.

Madness

mad·ness

/ˈmadnəs/

noun

1. What my world descended into

The Gifted Kid Burnout

I feel as though I need to <u>recreate greatness.</u>
What do you do when the heartbreak becomes so
repetitive that my (art) becomes so as well?
Art imitates life, yes?
And so what will my hands do when it no
longer feels the need to hold up the world?

I will be great, or I will be nothing. *But what if nothing IS great?*

I hate to think that this is it. It can't be. It can't
end here. What will my eyes do when it no longer
has the need to harbor tears?

How do I learn to be great at nothing?

I cannot accept that my fire has burnt out
so quickly,
I feel as though my empty hands must hold the
weight of the world.
I will not accept that.

I will be great, for I cannot be nothing.

She was the kind of fire
you'd want to hold and
the kind of heart you'd want
to break just to see if it would bleed.

I waited for the adventure,
I patiently sat there hoping for the
world to take me. But after waiting
forever, once again, stagnancy became
my only company.

I used to find refuge in sleeping;
it made me forget for just a couple hours. But over
time, my dreams betrayed me, and my nightmares
found a way to replicate my reality.

Perhaps I was so desperate to stay silent so that my pain did not have to be put so blatantly on paper.

The Moment Pain Became Generational

You never knew a kind world.
From the moment you opened your eyes, you were met
with violence. Life gave you nothing but scars, and the
world showed you nothing but pain. So without another
choice, you carry it with you and convinced yourself that
all of it was for good. So when that same world asked you
to be a parent, you silenced the screaming child within
you and convinced yourself that your anger was strength.
And with that, you met me with the same violence you've
known your whole life. You offered me pain because it
was the only thing you had. This was what made you;
this fire shaped you. So you burned me while the sounds
of my screams and wails echoed on. I begged you to stop,
but you weren't listening anymore. You stopped caring
a long time ago; you let the smoke cloud your eyes and
let the pain make you numb. I still cry for you at night;
I weep at the fact that it was never your fault. You were
hurting and no one came. You never knew a kind world,
so to survive, you made sure you were never kind at all.

All I ever wanted was to be the only child that was not the least favorite.

I saw myself standing in the crowd,
watching from across the room, not recognizing
my own voice as I speak full of passion and life.
Detachment had grasped onto me, and I no longer
saw the need to be with my own body.
What now?

—Future Diagnosed Dissociative
   Depersonalization Disorder.

And who are we to assume the people we worship wanted to be gods?

The worst part about showing promise is that sometimes you can't keep them.

The smudged ink had reminded her
of a time when being themselves
felt much clearer.

—Gender identity.

For a while I thought it didn't matter,
that unless my sadness turned into anger, I
wouldn't hurt anyone, and if I didn't hurt anyone,
they'd never turn to look.

My own voice started to hurt me.

"It's okay."
I said, wiping the blood.
My staggered breathing started to slow,
I picked up the pen that cut me, put it to paper,
and breathed,
"The more excruciating the pain,
the more the ink flows."

My walls started to suffocate me as
they've grown tired of hearing me speak
about how it hurts.

After all that, we wind up here again,
with my fear coming to life.
I'm starting to find comfort
in the blank stares again.

I never knew I could love my nightmares
more than I did my own reflection.

To think that after all this my world
would still be returned to me is
simply childish.

— What heartbreak has taught me.

So after you've beaten me, after
you are satisfied by how dark my bruises are, what
will you do with your hands then? Because god
knows you don't know how to hold me with them.

How do you heal from the knowledge
that the two people who were wired to
love you, never did?

Tell me, mom and Dad.
— ~~Questions from the daughter.~~

I looked down at my bloody hands,
My eyes wide, tears streaming down.
No. No, no, no.
I had hurt all of them in the way I swore I never
would. It was an accident, I swear. I feel a gentle
touch on my shoulder, the touch of their hands
made my neck tense.
Their voices echo,

"Good job darling,
we are so proud of you."

I never wanted to love like you.
You were the one thing I never wanted to be.
Because hearing someone say the
words I once said to you is one of the
worst kinds of pain.

So much growth,
I thought.
I've come so far.
But all of that was undone
the minute my mother said,

"You are just like your father."

And yet there she was, looking out the train window. Dreaming up all her fears and writing of things that would kill her.

You sat there staring at me as if I
suddenly meant nothing to you,

"How could you?"

I asked, fighting back a tear.

Your silence was enough of an answer.

The hope of every parent is to see their child let go of their hands and hold their own. But as I walked away, you griped my arms tighter, knowing that if you ever let go, I would see every scar from the times you made me bleed.

I sat in my dimly lit room as the sun set, the quiet taking over. I hear friends laughing in the living room just a door away. Yet I will always deny myself of such happiness, for then it is easier to let the sadness go.

I learned your kind of love; I carefully studied
how you showed affection and tailored myself to
it. I was desperate for any kind of love from you,
but you never learned my kind of love. I was your
daughter, but that didn't really matter, did it?

Ink from my pen overflows; it stains the paper, desperate to put meaningful words after the other. Just yesterday, it was stagnant, it refused to give me the release of writing. Now, one gentle touch to the paper and it bleeds, as if it has been keeping all the unsaid words, waiting to overflow.

—I

I hadn't picked up my pen in so long that it no longer fits the dent on my hand, the ink stains on my fingertips started to fade, I had forgotten what it was like to get lost in a fascinating world, and I don't know if I could ever find that again.

—II

The world had suddenly just brightened,
no light to find in the dullness anymore. I had no
pain to write of, yet simultaneously, the pain was
far too great to transcribe. The pen and paper
refused to feel that kind of pain as well. It denied
me of that release. So, with that, I have learned
that the ink comes when it is right for itself. Not
when I wish it to be and certainly not when
others demand it. It will only come when it is
good for the pen and paper itself.

—III

Chaos looked me in the eyes and told
me I was the most beautiful thing it had ever seen,
and hearing that, feeling needed at that capacity,
that made me stay.

I've been trying to stay afloat for so long, hoping that one day the currents will no longer want me dead.

I'd tell you that I have learned
how to keep it at bay, that it doesn't
suffocate me every night.
But I'm already lying to myself,
no use trying to convince another.

It's rushing over me now, shoving me
further and further down. Suffocating my free will
and killing my individuality.

After inhaling the idea that I have lost myself, my
lungs will no longer be
satisfied by air alone. So I will sit calmly as I
wait for the tide to take me, hoping that maybe
this time, I will be drowned by my own soul.

The Dark Room

All I wanted was to write you a Mother's Day card.
Yet here we are again, you on the other side of
the door you just locked, and me, desperately
scraping against it, my height not quite tall
enough to reach the doorknob. The lights are
off, it's been hours, I wonder if you'd leave me in
here overnight again. It was pitch black, even
after eleven years of being shoved in this room,
my eyes still haven't adjusted. Half my life was
spent curled up against that door, huddling to the
closest source of light. But over time, the horrors
behind that door stopped bothering me. As I grew,
you didn't have to forcefully drag me in kicking
and screaming. I wasn't three anymore, I had
been trained to walk myself into the trauma. But
I suppose I should thank you, because of all that,
I made a dear friend. The Darkness taught me
everything you didn't. It taught me how to love
differently, and most importantly, it taught me
that this wasn't love.

I learned it all on my own,
How to care for myself,
How to hold my heart,
And ultimately,
       How to love you.
So, through all the tears
and endless years,
I can finally sit here and say,
I forgive you.

—The Prodigal Parents.

How did you get here?
How did you allow books
to know your child's fears
more than yourself?

How could I be expected
to love myself when my
own hands remind me of
ones I've had to shield
myself from?

— I look too much like you.

My heart broke the minute I realized that the way I care for others is the same way you do too.

Feeling fictional started to make
itself familiar in my head.

My eyes started to space out,

Reality drifted further and further away.

I detached from my body as the
voices got more muffled.

I sat across myself, analyzing the way I spoke.

It felt so surreal I could almost hold my
own hands.

How do I stop it? How do I ground
myself when the rest of the world floats?

Yet after all the times that my core has been
crushed without my permission,
here I am, giving you my soul again.

Why wouldn't I know myself so well?

The parents I knew were the ones
who barely knew themselves.

I would take it day by day,
but every year, December 9th arrives.
I spend the day trying to find you, trying to feel
that unmatched warmth you used to radiate. I
take it back to the phone calls I missed, to the
times you held me tight when things got too
much. You were the first to tell me everything
was going be okay, and it was the last thing I said
to you. My mother lost a sister, my grandmother
lost a daughter, and I lost a best friend.

It wasn't that I never knew
what home was,
It was that home, to me,
was a place where
happiness was a privilege.

I stood on that stage, applause erupting and
bursting through the air. And in the crowd, all
I saw was her. The girl in the pink striped dress,
with two pigtails, smiling back at me.
Everything I've done, I did for her,
I only hope that she knows that.

All I can hope is that my hands
can hold up my world.
That this madness in the spring
will soon turn into an autumn of
senseless sanity,
and that one day, my soul will
find its way back to the pain that
made it feel alive.

Love

love

/ləv/

noun

1. What broke my core and
    simultaneously reshaped it

You broke me and chose to fix
someone else to make up for it.

If the world were fair,
Love would not have value at all.

You promised.
You looked me in the eyes
and promised that you would
never hurt me in such a way.
But if my parents have taught me
anything,
it's that a ring means *nothing*
in the eyes of a traitor.

Will you still love me when
you are no longer broken?

So we stood on that hill and made
promises laced with lies, swearing we would never hurt
each other, knowing full well that heartbreak
is our drug of choice.

I long for the days when
your eyes didn't tell a story of
regret every time you saw me.

One day,
when my love for you becomes
much greater than my own heart,
I will have the courage to let you go.

I keep taking myself back to the moment
right before you admitted to your actions, when
without a single word, your eyes had already told
me you broke a promise.

The light I had assigned to you
was dimming. Somewhere along the line,
you became friends with the dark too.

I had never known true heartbreak
until all I wanted to do was sleep.

—An insomniac's soliloquy.

It hurts to love you now.
But my mind keeps trying to
replicate what it was like before.
So here I am, telling you that I love you.

"How do you live with the
knowledge that the person you
love could still be yours again?"

*"By reminding yourself that they were never yours to
love in the first place."*

I started smiling at someone else's
words today.
Somehow that hurt more than
the heartbreak.

Being friends with someone you were
once in love with is like asking the
moon to be pulled by the sun's gravity
instead of Earth's.
It would burn, and the earth
would wither away.

JULY 19th, 2021

I SLEPT IN YOUR SHIRT TONIGHT,
SOMEHOW THE SCENT OF OUR
INTERTWINED LAUGHTER HAD
ALREADY STARTED TO FADE.

I feel like days have passed when
we've only hung up this morning.

I mended my heart piece by piece,
All whilst every shard still had your
reflection in them.

You had to start making excuses for me, that should have driven me enough to leave. I'm so sorry, I'll always be sorry.

Writing about you started to come
easily again—that was the moment
I knew I lost you.

How on earth am I supposed to breathe
when the air around me is poisoned by
the lies I told you?

—The art of blaming yourself for
something that was never your fault.

So it has been declared,
her heart will let her love
everything but him,
and he will be destined
to love her forever.

How did we get here?
How did unloving me become
such a simple task?

I know it wasn't my fault,
but I'm going to spend the rest of
my life wondering what I did wrong.

I hate you every day for leaving me
loving you more than I ever have.

But in the end,
after all the fighting,
she chose you.
　　　Love chose you.
We played the game, and I lost.
　　　So Love chose you to live, and I
have a feeling she will always choose
someone else but me to live.

My body felt foreign to the extra space
on the bed. I reached over, expecting you to be
there. But my hands found nothing but an imprint
of you and heartbreak.

It was a privilege to have my heart
broken by you and an honor
to have hated you.
Even after all this.

I try to walk away but it's like
my heart is still left behind,
    still in your hands,
        right where I left it.

So before we go off into our respective
futures, I know that you'll always keep a light on
for me, and I'll always sleep on one side of the bed
for you.

I was ready to stay forever,
yet it only took two hours and forty-two minutes
for you to walk away.

He managed to send me back to square
one with just a sentence, and for that, I will hate
them forever.

"I'm not ready for this right now."

Yet there you stand,
ready to try with her.

The worst kind of pain I had to learn a
lesson from was that I didn't deserve
your forgiveness, but you kept forgiving me over
and over. Until one day, my pain cost me you.

I have learned that one should never have to excuse pain in the name of soulmates.

I don't miss you.
I don't look for you in songs,
I don't think of your voice anymore,
and I don't look through our pictures.
But on some days, I still get your order at the coffee shop
because I'm not quite ready to let you go.

The hardest thing

You left like it was the easiest thing in the world. Easier than writing love letters, easier than having your heart be cared for by someone else, and easier than dying.

How cruel it was, that my guardian angel taught me that my kind of love will always be the kind to fall short, always be second best, and always be temporary.

I can only hope that you and I are not
meant to be. For the pain of losing you is far too
great. I told you I love you; I can only hope that
you believe me. I promise, I love you. God, I love
you. You must believe me.

I loved you.

But it's okay if you leave, I'll be okay. I promise.
And because I want to be okay, I can only hope
that you and I were not meant to be.

One of the most beautiful parts of love is what happens before you realize its blade has struck you. That split second, that in-between moment, when the feeling hits you, and everything seems to be detached from gravity then falls into the right place.

But what if it hurts?
What if I'm ~~wrong~~ again?
The last time I thought it was right, my heart was ripped
out of me and returned in shattered pieces.
I want to be happy, so why am I
invalidating my growth?
All I know is that I can't go through that again. I want to
love you, but I will love you on my own time.

in my own time.

You didn't "love me in your own way,"
just admit that you never loved me at all.

PRICE MATCH:
- We offer a one-time price match for any item on PacSun.com within 10 days of purchase with an original receipt
- The item you are price matching must be currently available on PacSun.com in the same style, size, and color – we do not price match 'similar' or 'practically the same' items.

GIFT CARDS:
- Gift cards are not redeemable for cash except as required by state law.
- Gift cards cannot be used as credit or debit cards.
- Terms and conditions are subject to change without notice.
- To replace a lost, stolen, or damaged gift card, as long as you have the original purchase receipt of 19-digit Gift Card number, please call 1.877.372.2786

SPECIAL PRODUCT & BRAND LAUNCHES:
- Select limited release Product may not be available for returns or exchanges – Customers will be informed of this policy at the time of

Here's to the hopelessly in love, with the type of love that is hopeless

It started with simple things:
a missing "good morning" and
"good night," scarce "I love you's" and even rarer
displays of it. Our text messages were no longer
at the top of my phone, and I'm almost startled
to see your name pop up. Our pictures move
farther down, descending into time as I fill my
album with newer memories. You were a part of
my life, imprinted on it, even. So, when I miss you,
something I one day hope to not do so often, I will
start with the simple things.

You've become a stranger my heart was
once tied to, but it no longer knows you now;
for that, I'm grateful.

— I don't miss you anymore

I need to stop breaking my own heart just so that
you might love me again.

You thought the world of me
until suddenly, I was nothing.
So here I am, picking you apart, in hopes that
loving you would get harder.
The worst part of me still hopes that if you are
broken, maybe you will love me again.

   —Loving someone for so long
    toxicity becomes normal.

It's unfair, I feel like an intruder
in your life now. When did we become so
estranged? At what point did our hearts
decide to grow apart? I hate that I'm
moving on; it hurts to keep living after feeling that
kind of love. But I suppose that's all love is,
it's unfair.

You left like it was
the easiest thing in
the world.
Easier than writing
love letters, easier
than being held,
and easier than
dying.

I have come to have peace
with the fact that sometimes,
simply loving each other is not enough.

Someone once told me that love is the
most irrational thing in the world, but we do it
anyway. And since then, although the heartbreak
is unbearable, I have loved madly. For I would
never rob myself of such a beautiful way to feel
infinite.

Threshold

thresh·old
/'THreSH,(h)old/

noun

1. The start of the perilous journey to healing

So I'll lay my sword down,
retrace my steps.
Trying to find the person
I once liked living with.
I'll lay my sword down,
long enough to let you in.
Because I liked being alive once,
I just can't find when.

It hits me some days,
I lost myself.
In every capacity,
I lost myself.
I wandered aimlessly alone
for quite a while.
I could've lost my soul forever,
but here I am, doing one of the most
mundane things, and being alive.
When those days happen, days when
it hits me, I gently smile to myself,
because despite it all, I found a way
to dance with myself again.

And yet, I found it in me to forgive you. After all the pain, I could truly forgive you. It took everything in me to utter those words, but in that moment, growing was the only thing that mattered.

I hope you do not repeat
the same mistake with her.
She has the chance to be kind.
Take it.

—A half sister's wishes.

But I know I will not be satisfied until my tears have hit the ground, every drop of my blood bleeds dry, and every smile has faded. Because the pain is often too good not to feel.

And so now you laugh away every terrible memory, as if erasing the fact that every night I used to pray for you to be gifted a different daughter.

Isolation became the
most comforting thing.
Because eventually
I learned that my own
voice was the only thing
that didn't hurt.

I've learned that the ones who don't know how to hurt will hurt others just to watch them cry, and witness a release they wish they knew.

I suppose that's the uncharted aspects of existing. You never really know when to fall or fly. All you know is that you will fight for your heart, and I'd like to believe that is enough.

I can admit I know nothing.
All I know is that life is a book bound by love
and pain, two things that are often the same.
And at any moment, it could fall apart. But the
wonderful thing is that no matter how torn apart
the spine might be, it is a book written by not just
ourselves, but others we meet along the way. So
when I hand my book over for you to write, I ask
you to scribble as much as you please. Don't leave
anything out, not a single heartbreak, a moment of
happiness, or a sleepless night.
Because at the end of the day, without
this book, we know nothing.

I hope you know that as the sun must
always set, the good will always end.
It will hurt, it will always hurt, we simply grow out of
feeling it. At some point the numbness will take over, the
tears will flow with no choice, and your ceiling will forever
be bored of watching you stare at it. You will always be hit
with surges of pain you can feel through your fingertips,
you will watch as you start to lose yourself, and you will
pick up the phone only to set it back down. Yet through all
this, that resilient heart of yours will continue to love and
your soul will insist on living.

And so it returns, that feeling I know all too well. The kind makes your strength leave you in almost an instant. But this time, this time I live. This time I will choose to cry loudly and love freely.

I'm running,
my heart is racing,
I am outrunning this heartbreak.
I will not let it consume me
the way the other have.
I sprint toward the middle,
not knowing what awaits me.
I can only hope that growth will
meet me there.

I have ripped out many pages from my book. But yours was not one I thought I would ever have to do.

Everything in me tells me to leave you
be. To let go of the hands that broke my core. But
you are still a person. No matter how much you
hurt me, you are still one of heart and blood. And
after all the times I have been deprived of such
compassion, I know that now is not the time of
vengeance.

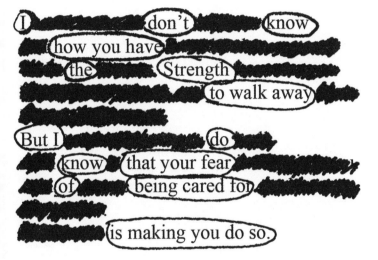

I don't know
how you have
the Strength
to walk away

But I do
know that your fear
of being cared for

is making you do so.

It hurt.
God it hurt.
Hearing your voice hurt,
Feeling you slip away hurt,
But losing myself hurt most.

I can see it clearly now,
the way that un-loving me came so
naturally to you explains it all.
It was because you were endless chapters in my
book, but I[1]

---

[1]was just a footnote.

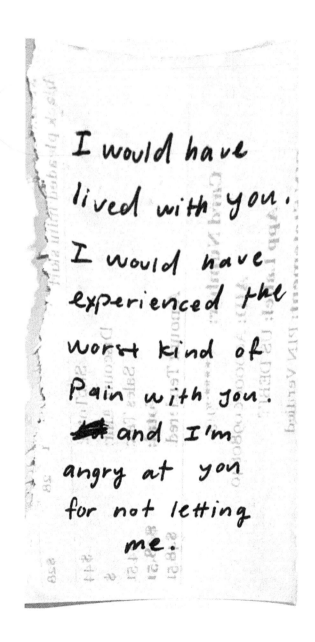

I would have
lived with you.
I would have
experienced the
worst kind of
Pain with you.
~~it~~ and I'm
angry at you
for not letting
me.

I had to lie to myself saying that it was all my fault because I didn't accept that you couldn't do it anymore.

For years I asked myself,

Why was I not worth staying?

Then I realized that they had to leave
because it was simply not right.
I am worth staying, but it just
wouldn't be right.

I want to hold you;
I want to feel your warmth again.
But I must find my own temperature first, for I know that
yours is powerful.

Your force wrecks everything in its path, and for me to be
there, I must find my ground.

So I left with you in my heart,
as I learn to feel my hand
when it is not in yours.

I grew,
through the fire,
I grew.
I fought for my heart,
I chased after my soul,
and I kept my mind loyal.
I am proud of what I've done,
I'm proud that I was able
to unlearn their hatred.

Entry of an Immigrant

I grew up with different pavements,
Ones with holes and cracks
I learned to jump over.
I grew up with different air,
One that made you sweat away
your fears and cough up your anger.
I grew up with a different love,
One that was conditional.
And a different pain,
One that was generational.
So now, six years and 8,995 miles later,
After living in another place with other people
to call home,
I must learn how to walk on new pavements,
breathe different air, and understand a
different love.

"So it's not an epic poem?"

I smiled, gently pushing the swing.

"No, it isn't."

She looks up at me and smiles.

"That's okay, epic poems turn out to be tragedies anyway."

I push the swing again, this time a little harder. I want to see her float, I want to see her fly.

"All you need to know is that we're happy."

As she rises in the air, the swing going forward, she doesn't look back this time.

"Good. That's good. That's more than enough."

"I'm sorry—god I'm so sorry"

I stumbled, breath shaking.
She cups my face as I fall at her feet.

"I just want to show you that it gets better, that
the sinking feeling goes away at some point."

She wipes a tear; I hold her small hand. She takes
me in and holds me there on the ground.

"You grew. You admitted that it will
always hurt, and you grew accustomed to
it. And for that, I'm proud of us."

I can finally
think about us without
my heart dropping.

The scars started to fade,
and for the first time,
I can allow them to do so.

Missing them became much more
powerful than loving them.

Grief stripped me down,
it touched my skin and concluded
that there was more to me.
It revealed how I hurt,
it forced me to learn how to heal,
and it introduced me to the idea of
loving a memory as if
it was the person themselves.

Walking away from home
was much easier than I thought.
And somehow, that hurt me.

It's okay to miss them.
It's okay to have your moments with
them be the defining moments of your
life. It's alright to grieve, and it's alright to say a
requiem. Moving on does not erase the value of
the time spent with them.

The storms might never pass,
the heartbreak will be endless,
and the sun could never rise.
But regardless, you,
resilient, capable, you.
You live, you always have, and you will. I'm so proud.

I hope you know that your
Soul is so beautiful to me that
I consider it to be art.

I held my enemy as she cried on the
battlefield, the blood on our hands
intertwined, both of us had lost enough.

Although I am not ready to speak
to you just yet, I am ready to heal.
I will hold my own hand through this,
And one day, perhaps I can meet your
eyes again without my heart breaking.

How do I know I'm ready?
What if I don't know myself
as well as I thought?

All you need to know is that
Life does not stop for you,
and you will never be ready for
anything. But it is in those moments
where growth happens.

I watched as the house burned down.
It's alright, I never knew home, it was
just a house.

Growth came from the shadows,
it intertwined up my legs and consumed
my heart. And before I knew it, healing
became easier.

To: Aurora

I am so proud of you.
You healed.
You lost her but you healed.
You lived through her death
and came out more resilient
than ever.
Your heart is just like hers,
and your mind is one she's
so proud of.
You have her kindness,
And you have her love.
I love you.
I know I don't say it often
but I love you.
You are worth more than
the stars, your heart shines
just like your name.
She's proud. I hope you know that.
And I, with everything I am,
I'm so proud of you.

Give me a minute.
I just need a second to breathe.
A moment to inhale,
A night to heal.
I will be okay, I will live.
I will live through it just like
I did the others.

"I don't feel safe around you anymore."

He said on that fateful Saturday night.

It took so long to unlearn, but I
understand it now.

"No. You simply never felt safe around yourself."

Depression became my partner,
it became a friend I never asked for.
But through all the times I've been hurt, it stayed. It was
the only consistent thing I knew. So I learned to care for
it, and eventually, live with it.

There is no such thing as too far gone,
I cannot accept that.
I will jump into the abyss for you even if it means
that I have a chance of getting you back. No one
deserves that little compassion. At the very least,
everybody deserves some
form of humanity.

I know we don't speak at all, but if the world was ending tonight, you'd still eat pancakes for dinner with me, right?

It took years for me to be able to hope
again. Your love—my first example of love—
permitted me to accept pain and abuse. I
normalized getting hurt; I justified the crimes.
Loving has become difficult because of you. I
spent ages telling myself it's all my fault.
I hate you. Because it took years for me to be
able to hope again.

The complicated aspect of healing is the idea that pain is all you really deserve.

Let go.
The weight of the world
is not yours to carry.
Let go.
I will help your hands heal.
Just let go for me.

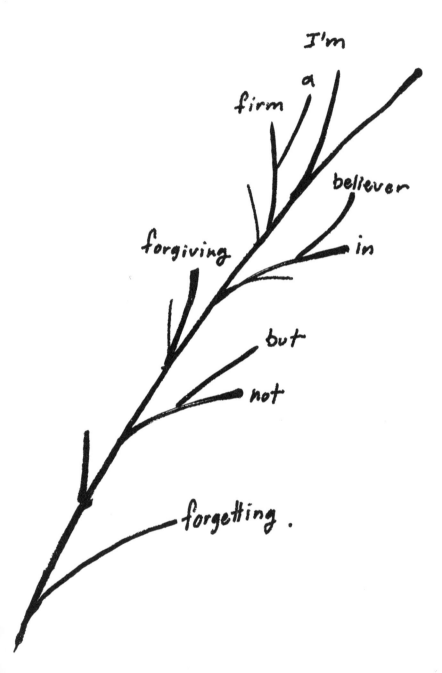

So you think that does it?!
One apology,
one apology suddenly erases
years of pain you caused me.
How dare you.
How dare you expect forgiveness
simply because you apologized.
No. You owe it to me to give me time.

This I have to do on my own.
I must build my own home.
I will build it brick by brick,
With the bittersweet memories,
The unforgettable moments,
And the euphoric heartbreaks.
You have done all you can,
This I have to do on my own.

Requiem

req·ui·em

/ˈrekwēəm/

noun

1. Memories that have shaped me

2. A collection from the books
   The Hard Part is Living and
   Uncharted Existence

Part I

The Hard Part is Living

"How was your day?"

"I almost didn't have one."

"Good, and you?"

I never really had nice handwriting, but I tried
to change.
Because maybe if I changed my
handwriting to be like her,

you'll love me like her too.

<u>City of Stars.</u>

I had forgotten what it felt like to overlook the
city, the city that has something everybody wants.
I fell in love with the warmth, the buildings, the
lights, and everything abnormal about this city. If
you look close enough, the alleyways have art, and
every person has that light in their eyes, the ones
you see when there's a promised dream.

No matter what happens here, the heartbreak or
the victory, I will always love it. I stood outside of
the observatory, and while others were looking
at the stars, I fell in love with the ground I walked
on. The city hugged me with passion and vibrance,
like a soundtrack to a timeless movie.
This is the city that many run to.
This is it.

This is home.
The bustling of the crowd started to fade behind
me, and I stood on that hill overwhelmed with
beauty because, oh right, it's lovely where I live.

So tell me,
how does one
unalign
the stars?

I have come to believe that it is our belief in a heavenly afterlife that makes our lives living hell.

There was never truly a
Good reason to stay,
Just a million reasons not
To go through with it.

She was in love with everything that
exhausted her.

She thought she had felt true exhaustion.
But she was wrong. It was this,

it was when being exhausted felt like a
tiresome activity.

At this point,
authentic happiness seems
far more artificial than faking it.

How selfish Life can be,
It will zip you around the universe
Then push you into the sun.
It will take you to lovely places
Then blind you for fun.
It will grab you by the heart and show you how to fly,
Then throw you off a cliff, leaving you to die.
And when it is done with you, it will throw you on
Death's door, broken, torn, and shaken to your core.
But Death will take you in
And hold you by the fire.
For it knows deep down,
That Life is a liar.
It will hold you so tight,
Even if you refuse.
It will not harm you one bit,
For it knows you have
nothing left to lose.

Exhausted of Life's yelling,
I answered the door.
And there stood Death,
waiting for me.

Death stood there in the moonlight,
and She was beautiful.

Mon, June 29, 2020

"Don't die on me, okay? That's all I'm asking. Please promise me."

"I won't, I'm better now."

Tue, June 30, 2020

"You promised."

She's trying, she really is.
It's just getting harder and harder,
to write with poison ink and put her life on paper.
She is trying to fix herself, drawing little hearts
and stars, strategically placing them on her arm,
over the cuts and scars. So please understand that
it is hard to go farther, it is hard for her to live, in a
world that has lost its wonder.

I was alone.
Completely and utterly alone.
I was silent and lonely,
With no one around to see.
So don't tell me I was wrong
To take the hands of Death,
For I was alone,
And Death showed me kindness.

She stood across her and asked,

"Why do you take so long to come for me?"

Death smiled,
"You're quite impatient.
Others spend their lives
trying to outrun me."

She looked at Death longingly and said,

"I've met Life,
I wasn't impressed."

I had found out the truth a long time ago, the moment life hit, that I was one to write of love but never truly know it.

<u>In Fear of Falling in Love.</u>

I made sure I didn't ruin anything.
I taught myself to say the right things. I made sure
that we were never alone; I made sure I didn't
laugh too hard at your jokes. I did it all.
I made sure that I wouldn't look at you for too
long in fear of falling in love.
I didn't tell you because I knew that
you'd do anything for me.
You would do anything to make me happy
because you cared.
If I told you I loved you, you would try so hard to
love me too.
But you won't, because you can't. Then you'd lie
to yourself and say that you love me too. For you
are too stubborn to admit that love cannot be
summoned, and you will keep trying because that
is your way.

It's one of the most painful things,
to watch two people who once vowed to spend
the rest of their lives together,

become complete strangers.

It's alright, I think I already knew. It's not your fault the pain is real. The heartbreak was too fateful to be false.

The wishing wells will not do you any
good, the stars you wish on will not fix you, and
the four-leaf clovers will not help you. But the
fires you learn to dance on, the storms you know
to weather, and the summers you spend alone will
teach you how to love.

So I depart with you this:
May the darkness find you,
May the brightness blind you,
And may the love sting you.
For it is then, when you will learn to fall in love
with being alive all over again.

Part II

Uncharted Existence

I hope you frame the loss
and cherish the hurt.
For the victories do not need
to outshine what truly makes you.

Her.

So she found it, the very meaning of the night sky she loved so much. She hardly hopes and hopes to hurt. The night sky was nothing more than just that, but to her, it meant teaching herself to see in the dark again. In every star, she saw the times she fought, and in every particle of dark matter, she saw the times she lost. She lived like she wanted no tomorrow, she loved like no one had seen, and she hoped that one day the world would pick her out of the bunch and show her the secrets of the stars. She wanted to be loved as much as she did the moon, she wanted someone to see her the way she saw dark matter, and she wanted for someone to find the very meaning of who they are in her like she does the night sky. She was a stranger to the ground she laid on; her eyes were of sunsets eager to touch the stars. She had found it, right there, right here.

The very meaning of the night sky she loved so much.

I knew I would lose it.
I knew one day it would all be gone.
So before that happens,
I will teach you how to love,
I will show you how I live,
And I will write you the unexplainable.
I will teach you how to say goodbye.

You are every wonderful story, every painful metaphor, and all the brightest colors, put together, all at once, released into the world.

Everything?

There is so much of everything,
I don't know how to tell you there is.
But I want it all, I want to take it all. I want to
breathe everything in even if I don't have the
capacity for it. So give me the dark nights, give
me the papercuts, give me the sunsets, give me
the laughter, and give me the kind of pain that
paralyzes you. Because I will feel it all just for the
sake of experiencing my mortality in the most
infinite way I can.

She wanted to transcend every feeling of pain she had ever felt, or rather, the excessive amounts of it, onto paper. She wished that for once she could read her story like a book, one that could never truly harm her but make her feel all the same.

And who are we to assume that the sun prefers to
be the center of our universe?

"And who might you be?"
asked the White Rabbit,
"I'm the girl who is madly in love with a world
that will never love her the same."

I was angry,
angry at a world that gave me a curse but taught
me to love it as a miracle.

Su*c!de Note.

The pen glides against the paper, as if it was urging her to write her final words just a little faster.

I'm not asking you to fight, I'm asking you to breathe. Because although fighting may be more satisfying, breathing is just as hard.

A Bottle of Pills.

She was the kind to fidget with life and death
between her fingers.
The familiar rattle of her memories echoed in
the dark. She toyed with the idea of letting the
small bottle take her. She twirled it between her
fingers as the control she had over it gave her an
unmatched euphoria.

"Why?" Some might ask.

Because she knows she cannot convince
herself to wake up tomorrow morning.

I met them when I was just a young girl, they stood in front of me, extending their hand.

"Hello," they spoke.

"I'm Darkness,
and I will be your dearest friend."

I am fortunate enough to say that growing up has taught me that eventually, the Darkness will be my hero.

I stay up late, sometimes all night, trying to piece together the world, only to take it all apart and hoping to call it art.

I never blamed the Dark for
the absence of my childhood.
For it was the Light that
stole it from me.

"Take care of her,"
Life said gently.
"Of course, my dear,
I always do." Death smiled.
Life gave a sad smile.
"I'm sorry I won this time."
said Death,
"It's all right,"
Life smiled,
"I don't mind losing to you, my love."

The candle was burning out. I gently
shielded it from the wind with my hand.
Without it I won't know where I'm going. But as
it faded away, I knew, I had no choice but to grow
accustomed to the dark.

You loved me, and I loved you,
but my pen didn't like us on paper.

Love was not what I thought it would be,
It shifted, changed, hurt,
But for the first time,
Love was something
I didn't mind running after.

The stars will never know you
if they never meet your eyes,
the oceans will never hear your voice if you never
scream, and the earth will never feel you
if you never cry.

For 16 Years.

You taught me to forgive,
but it took me a while to realize,
that you taught me to forgive
over and over because you wanted me to
keep forgiving you over and over.
Even if it killed me.

How do I do this?
Teach me how to accept this kind of love when my
definition of it has always been violence.

<u>(Bad) Parenting</u>.

Teach me how to unlearn everything you've taught me, tell me how to untie the ropes you taught me to weave, and show me how to die better than I lived.

Will it still be requital then?
Your love for me?

Will you still be here
when I am no longer broken?

I never asked much of you;
I never hoped to see you at Christmas. And yet when I
hear your footsteps down the hall, I flinch just a little.

The ink will stain your hands; they will mark them with all the painted tragedies and untold victories.

And by the end of it all, there will be a story you will want to tell.

Échec et mat (Checkmate).

I meticulously moved the pieces one by one, strategically looking for the moves that would not harm me, hoping that a catalyst would never arrive. The black and white squares are taunting me now, and you moved a simple pawn. I wasn't sure if that was a plan to kill or nothing at all. I see a window to attack and perhaps even kill. But I looked at you, and your eyes told me the game wasn't meant to be over, not yet. We kept moving them, placing them in corners we thought the other would never find. The pieces glided as we danced across the board, Wanting to take our time to the inevitable outcome. Every time I hit the clock, my heart rate rose as if my whole body knew the brutal endgame was next. You moved that pawn again, then I saw it. The fatal move that could end this all. The music dimmed, time stopped, and my eyes froze. I sat there, eyes glued on your King. This was not what I wanted for us. I tried to meet your eyes, and they were filled with the kind of fear I knew all too well. Your eyes begged me to make the kill quick and painless. So I gently picked up my Queen and softly set it next to your King. We both knew this was it. I watched as you gently laid your King down; the thud of the piece hitting the board was jarring. You got up and smiled, but before you left, you slipped the pawn into your pocket. I knew I would never play anyone like you ever again. Deep down, I knew the cost was far too great. This time, the checkmate wasn't worth it.

She has given so much of herself away, that she doesn't have much of herself left. So even the bad and the painful, she now keeps near.

I now know why storms are named after people.

"How does that make you feel?"

It doesn't.

"Hurt, I guess?"

I tried to shift in my bed
to make myself more comfortable,
comfortable enough to say goodbye.
I held my breath trying to build up the
courage to tell you.
You said nothing,
and for a moment, I wish you did.
I wish you fought; I wish I fought.

But the fact that neither of us
tried to stay said it all.

I hate you for making me hate the only part of me
I have taken so long to learn to love.

It will hurt,
you will bleed,
it will be unbearable, and you will scream.
But I promise you,
it will be worth it.
All the sleepless nights, ceiling views,
empty hands,
and broken trusts. Because one day
you will see,
that you are worth
so much more than infinity.